DUNE FOX

Written and illustrated by

Marilynne K. Roach

An Atlantic Monthly Press Book

Little, Brown and Company

Boston   Toronto

FIRST EDITION

T 09/77

Library of Congress Cataloging in Publication Data

Roach, Marilynne K.
    Dune fox.

    "An Atlantic Monthly Press book."
    SUMMARY: Follows the activities of a fox living
on the dunes and describes the plant and animal
life that he encounters throughout the seasons.
    1. Red fox—Juvenile literature. 2. Sand
dune ecology—Juvenile literature. [1. Red fox.
2. Foxes. 3. Sand dune ecology. 4. Ecology]
I. Title.
QL737.C22R6   599'.74442   76-54755
ISBN 0-316-74870-6

ATLANTIC-LITTLE, BROWN BOOKS
ARE PUBLISHED BY
LITTLE, BROWN AND COMPANY
IN ASSOCIATION WITH
THE ATLANTIC MONTHLY PRESS

*Published simultaneously in Canada
by Little, Brown & Company (Canada) Limited*

PRINTED IN THE UNITED STATES OF AMERICA

FOX ran along the dunes. A low mist of skipping sand stung his nose. The sand lay unmarked before him and the wind smoothed away his tracks behind.

SPARROW HAWK

Fox lived on one of the islands in the nearby salt marsh and often hunted on the dunes. He knew them in every weather and in every season.

Fox paused beside a cut trampled through the lip of a certain dune. The wind blew across it, carrying no hint of the creature that had made the original track.

POISON IVY

COCKLEBUR

In the beginning mountains
rose from the earth's fiery heart.

Those mountains were worn
by winds and long-gone glaciers.
Pebbles and silt washed down their
sides into rivers and to the sea.

The ceaseless waves
ground them down to sand.

Cast up on beaches, the
grains dried and blew inland
to form the dunes.

Over the dune a colony of terns nested on the sand. Fox stood downwind in a clump of cocklebur on a ridge and eyed a certain nest.

He dashed forward. The birds rose in a screaming cloud and

dived to peck him hard, to drive him from the unfledged chicks. He ran through the confusion of wings and doubled back over the dunes with a mouthful of eggs. Screaming birds pursued him across the hot sand.

The pale sand, quartz flecked with garnet, reflected so fierce a heat that some plants curled their leaves to keep from drying out. Fox headed for the shade of the cedar swamp, catching and eating as he went a few of the scurrying insects. He snapped at the sand-colored grasshoppers which leaped high above the burning surface. The greenhead flies bit at Fox, and he hurried on.

He passed a little bembex wasp burying her eggs underground in cooler sand. From time to time she hovered in the cooler air above the surface to keep from cooking as she worked. In shaded hollows, wolf spiders ran down unwary beetles, and ant lions lurked at the bottoms of their pit-traps.

SICKLE-LEAVED GOLDEN ASTER

DUSTY MILLER

SEA ROCKET

SEABEACH SANDWORT

SEASIDE GRASSHOPPER

BEMBEX WASP

ANT LION

GREEN HEAD FLY

TIGER BEETLE

WOLF SPIDER

WORMWOOD

9

In the cool of evening, Fox headed from the swamp, up past the scrub oak to where the sand drifted from the dunes into the pines. He crept among the sumac and beach plums on the back dunes and dashed after a rabbit into a hollow full of roses.

It veered up the foredunes and he nearly brought it down in a cluster of poverty grass. But the rabbit twisted away and escaped into a tangle of poison ivy. The ivy grew everywhere, creeping under the sea wind and into the hollows, and swarming up the trees on the edge of the woods.

The next rabbit was not so swift.

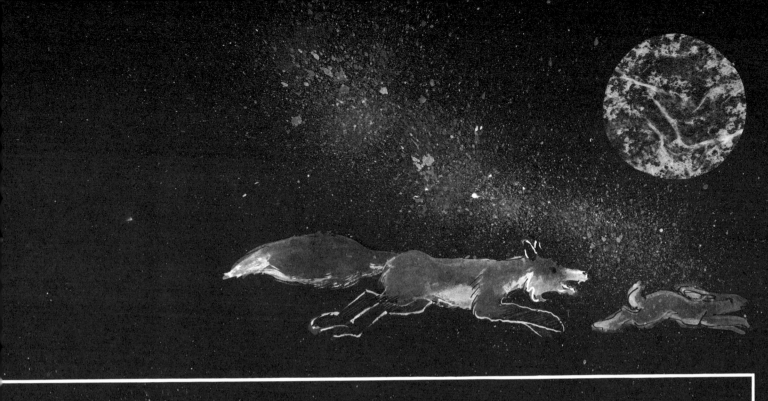

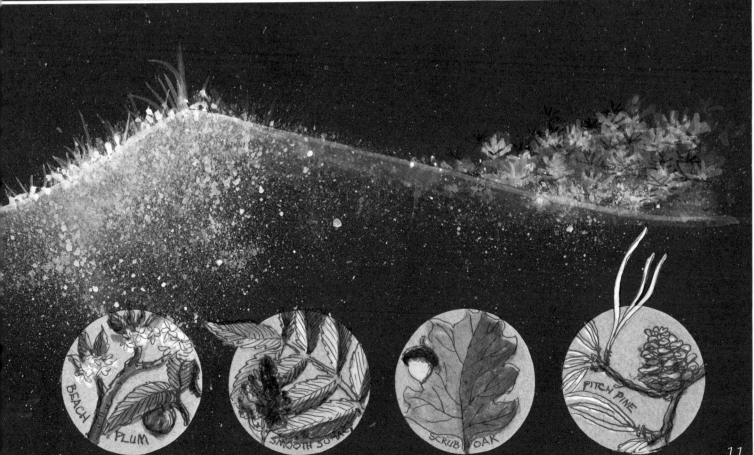

JOINTWEED

BROOM CROWBERRY

WATER TABLE

POND

POND

BOBWHITE

PINWEED

Sometimes on still days, a salt-scented fog spread out of the sea over the dunes and marshlands, filling the cedar swamps and reaching the uplands. It beaded all the leaves with a dew that brushed off on Fox's fur as he passed.

Fungi appeared and even the earth stars, those movable mushrooms, unfolded their points and held still.

The plants and the sand itself absorbed the moisture. The little ponds in the hollows that had dried during the summer reappeared as the water table rose.

EARTH STAR

Autumn brought a briskness to the winds that rushed over the still-warm dunes. Fox was nearly hit on the nose with a free-rolling earth star, dried now and casting its spores out into the world.

Poison ivy and bearberry leaves had become crimson. The grasses were copper and gold and reflected shining arcs of light along the sweep of their stalks. Fox cautiously sniffed a toad crouched under the waxy clusters of a bayberry bush and settled for ripe beach plums instead.

The bright sky was full of migrating birds, and flights of monarch butterflies hurried south over the dunes.

HOG-NOSED
SNAKE

MONARCH BUTTERFLY

BEACH PLUM

BAY BERRY

FOWLER'S TOAD

BEARBERRY

POISON IVY

15

Early winter rains soaked and pitted the dunes. Winds drove the ocean tides over the beach and onto the foredunes. The roaring of waves was loud even in distant sheltered hollows.

The sands drank up the cold rain and stored it deep among the grains — in roots and covered vegetation, in buried rotting trees — against the next summer's dryness. The surface was marked with footprints as it dried.

A band of deer moved nervously among the hollows, and Fox watched the large animals from his ridge.

17

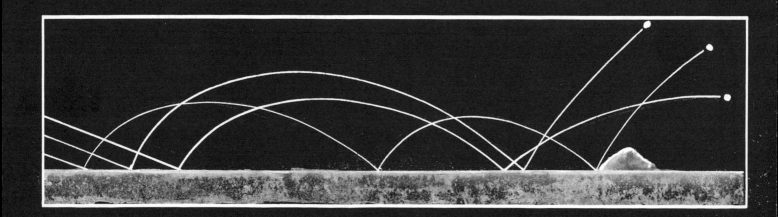

The dunes walked farther with the wind as the nights grew longer. Grain by grain the sand blew off the lips and fell into the hollows, farther and farther across the outer lands. The peaks moved and the hollows moved, and the wind's passing marked ridges in the dunes' flanks.

Fox turned his tail to the plumes of sand that streamed in the wind from the deepening cut. The air seemed always full of sand.

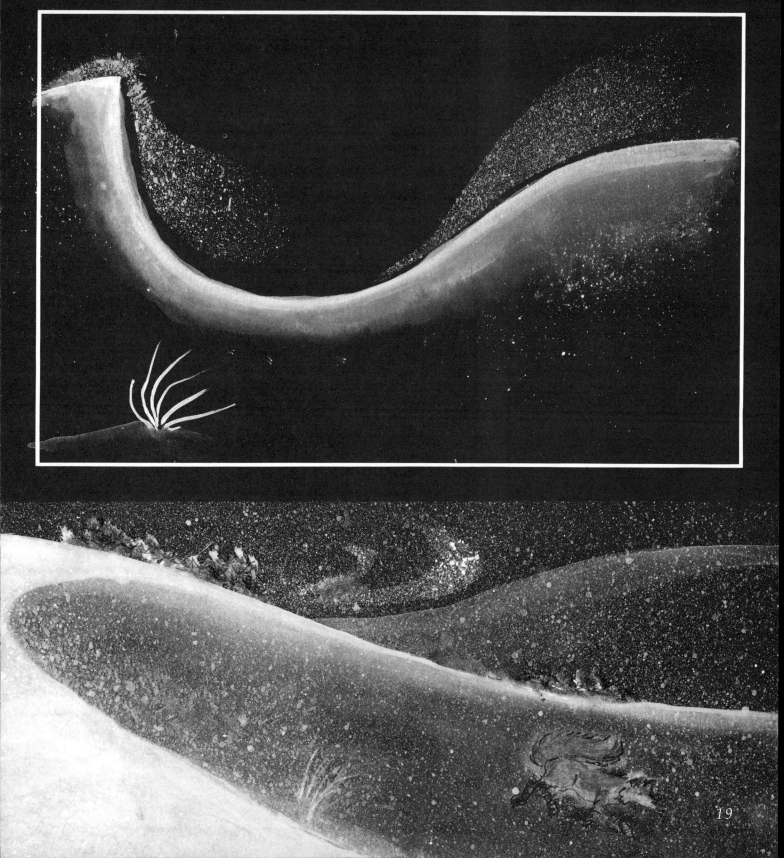

19

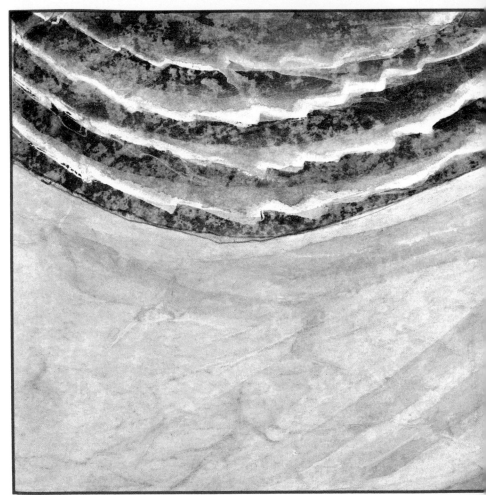

Tempests came screaming over the ocean and gouged tons of earth from the tall cliffs on another part of the coast. Currents carried the new sand and deposited it at the end of a sandbar near Fox's marsh.

Fox waited out the storms in protected hollows, curled up with his tail over his nose. Dens were for cubs. He stayed above ground, huddled until the sun broke through the storm clouds.

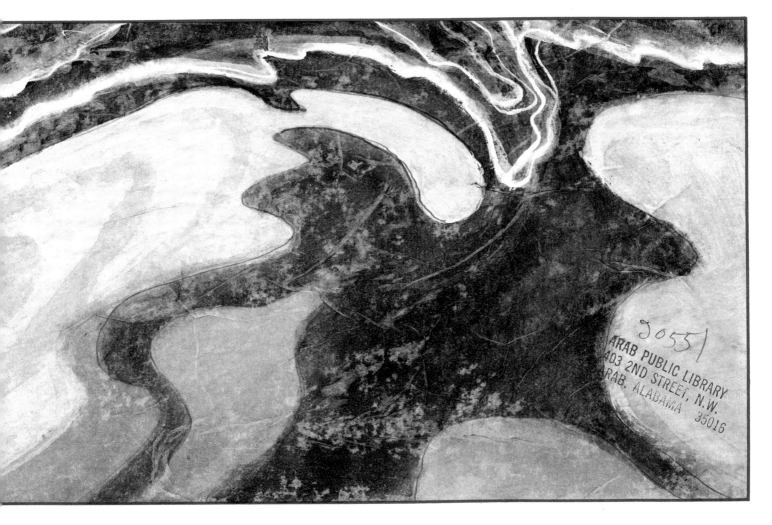

21

SNOW BUNTINGS

Some of the dunes were gone, shifting with the gales, and blown grain by grain into new sand dunes in new places. The wind had twisted around other dunes to whittle them away without pushing them forward. Still others, like Fox's favorite ridge, were well anchored by layers of dead vegetation and the strong roots of living plants. These dunes had changed shape but, held fast, had not moved. All were edged with snow.

Fox, ravenous after the long storm, spotted a dead rabbit at the base of a snow pile. He made a snatch, but the pile opened golden eyes and hissed. It was a snowy owl.

Fox ran hungrily over the barren sand. A gull and crow were quarreling over a fish caught among the bones of a long-dead whale. While they fought, Fox stole the fish.

CROW

HERRING GULL

A March storm blew dovekies ashore by the hundreds. Those few who could creep to water got back into the air. Their short legs were for swimming, and set so far back on their bodies that the birds were nearly helpless on land. They were true seabirds who wintered in the air and on the sea.

Fox sat on his favorite ridge and gorged on dovekies. Below the sand was buried snow, beneath the snow more sand and buried beach grass. The roots of the grass were living still and waiting for spring, when they would send up new shoots.

DOVEKIE

BRANT   GREATER SCAUPS   COMMON EIDERS   OLD-SQUAWS

A last furious winter storm ended in a south wind, and with it came flocks of restless birds. The shrubs in the dunes and the channels of the marsh were loud with their calling.

The wind carried young caterpillars that humped along where the buried beach grasses rose again from the sands. Shoots and buds appeared in all the crests and hollows, on the salt-loving plants of the outer beach, and the protected shrubs behind the heights of sand.

Fox ate the sweet green buds. The shrew he chased proved too quick, but he devoured an early nest of tender mice.

MEADOW MOUSE

CANADA GOOSE

BEACH PLUM

SKUNK

SHORT-TAILED SHREW

TENT CATERPILLAR

SEASIDE GOLDENROD

BEACH PEA

28

In the winter's storms the sea had broken completely through the cut, and the terns now nested on a mound which had become an island. Fox sat on his ridge watching the birds huddled among the beach peas and goldenrod. They had less room than last year, but they did have a moat. Perhaps at low tide he would try wading through the channel.

Now he trotted back to the marsh to catch crabs. The wind blew sand over the footprints he left behind him.

Notes

This introduction to a year's cycle on the dunes could take place in any number of sites along the northeast coast. This fictional shore area, however, is an idealized combination of several places on Cape Cod.

While the constant changes of life and death within nature are meant to be present, it is assumed this imaginary area is free of guns, motor vehicles, traps, litter, poisons, landfill, and other examples of human interference.

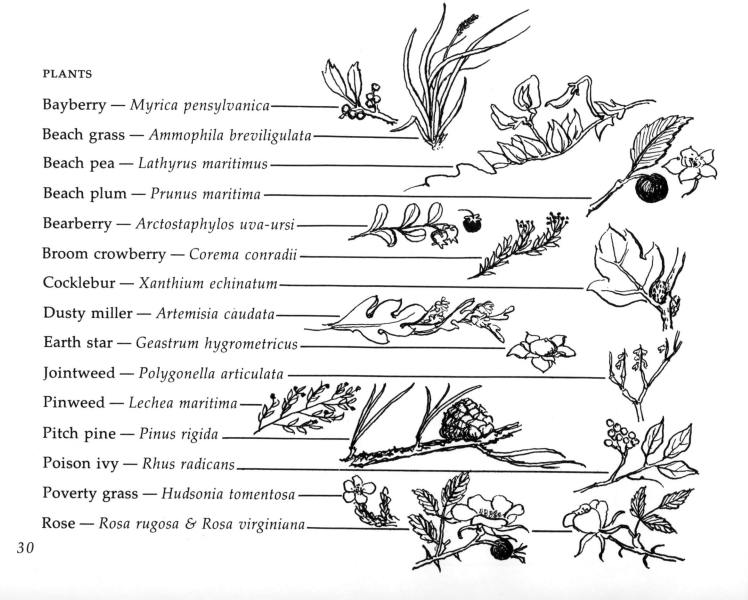

PLANTS

Bayberry — *Myrica pensylvanica*

Beach grass — *Ammophila breviligulata*

Beach pea — *Lathyrus maritimus*

Beach plum — *Prunus maritima*

Bearberry — *Arctostaphylos uva-ursi*

Broom crowberry — *Corema conradii*

Cocklebur — *Xanthium echinatum*

Dusty miller — *Artemisia caudata*

Earth star — *Geastrum hygrometricus*

Jointweed — *Polygonella articulata*

Pinweed — *Lechea maritima*

Pitch pine — *Pinus rigida*

Poison ivy — *Rhus radicans*

Poverty grass — *Hudsonia tomentosa*

Rose — *Rosa rugosa & Rosa virginiana*

Scrub oak — *Quercus ilicifolia*

Seabeach sandwort — *Arenaria peploides*

Sea rocket — *Cakile edentula*

Seaside goldenrod — *Solidago sempervirens*

Sickle-leaved golden aster — *Chrysopsis falcata*

Smooth sumac — *Rhus glabra*

Wormwood — *Artemisia caudata*

ARACHNIDS

Wolf spider — *Lycosa pikei*

INSECTS

Ant lion — *Myrmeleon immaculatus*

Bembex wasp — *Bembex spinolae*

Greenhead fly — *Tabanus nigrovittatus*

Monarch butterfly — *Danaus plexippus*

Seaside grasshopper — *Trimerotropsis maritima*

Tent caterpillar (gypsy moth) — *Malacosoma americanum*

Tiger beetle — *Cicindella hirticollis*

AMPHIBIANS

Fowler's toad — *Bufo fowleri*

REPTILES

Eastern hog-nosed snake — *Heterodon platyrhinos*

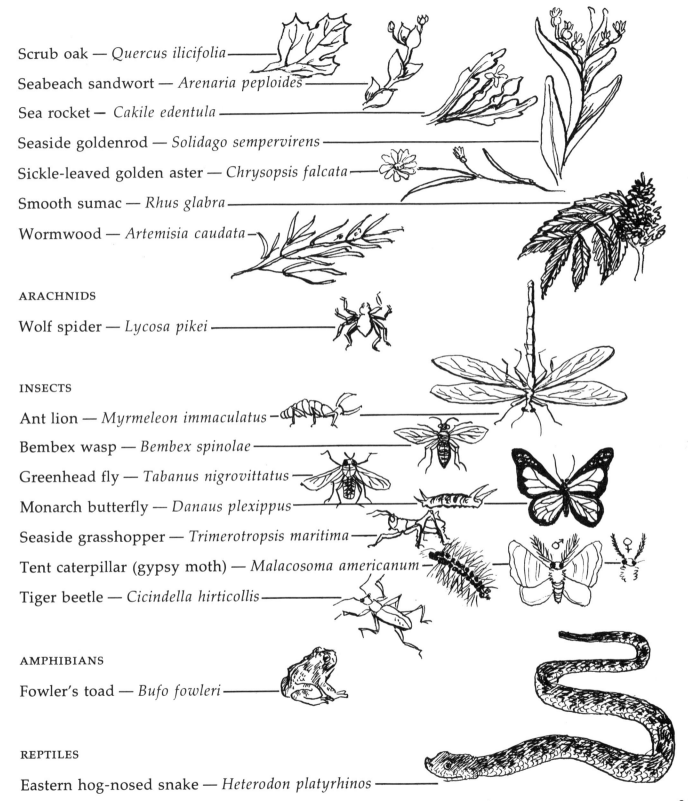

BIRDS

Bobwhite — *Colinis virginianus*

Brant — *Branta bernicla*

Canada goose — *Branta canadensis*

Common crow — *Corvus brachyrhynchos*

Common eider — *Somateria mollissima*

Common tern — *Sterna hirundo hirundo*

Dovekie — *Plautus alle*

Greater scaup — *Aythya marila nearctica*

Herring gull — *Larus argentatus*

Old-squaw — *Clangula hyemalis*

Snow bunting — *Plectrophenax nivalis*

Snowy owl — *Nyctea scandiaca*

Sparrow hawk — *Falco sparverius*

MAMMALS

Eastern cottontail rabbit — *Sylvilagus floridanus*

Meadow mouse — *Microtus pennsylvanicus*

Raccoon — *Procyon lotor*

Red fox — *Vulpes fulva*

Short-tailed shrew — *Blarina brevicauda*

Skunk — *Mephitis mephitis*

White-tailed deer — *Odocoileus virginianus*